MAZE RUNNER:
THE
SCORCH TRIALS™

OFFICIAL GRAPHIC NOVEL PRELUDE

MAZE RUNNER: THE SCORCH TRIALS OFFICIAL GRAPHIC NOVEL PRELUDE Scholastic Edition, June 2015. Published by BOOM! Studios, a division of Boom Entertainment, Inc. Maze Runner: The Scorch Trials is © 2015 Twentieth Century Fox Film Corporation. All rights reserved. BOOM! Studios™ and the BOOM! Studios logo are trademarks of Boom Entertainment, Inc., registered in various countries and categories. All characters, events, and institutions depicted herein are fictional. Any similarity between any of the names, characters, persons, events, and/or institutions in this publication to actual names, characters, and persons, whether living or dead, events, and/or institutions is unintended and purely coincidental. BOOM! Studios does not read or accept unsolicited submissions of ideas, stories, or artwork.

For information regarding the CPSIA on this printed material, call: (203) 595-3636 and provide reference RICH# – 619781. A catalog record of this book is available from OCLC and from the BOOM! Studios website, www.boom-studios.com, on the Librarians Page.

BOOM! Studios, 5670 Wilshire Boulevard, Suite 450, Los Angeles, CA 90036-5679. Printed in USA. First Printing.

ISBN: 978-1-60886-786-8, eISBN: 978-1-61398-457-4

"WORLD GONE WICKED"

Written by Jackson Lanzing & Collin Kelly
Art by Tom Derenick
Colors by Whitney Cogar
Letters by Jim Campbell

Designer: Kelsey Dieterich
Associate Editor: Whitney Leopard
Editor: Dafna Pleban

From the world of the 20th Century Fox Feature Film
MAZE RUNNER: THE SCORCH TRIALS

Written by T.S. Nowlin

Based on the novel by James Dashner

Produced by Wyck Godfrey, Marty Bowen,
Ellen Goldsmith-Vein, Lee Stollman, and Joe Hartwick Jr.

Directed by Wes Ball

Special thanks to Wes Ball, T.S. Nowlin, Wyck Godfrey, Cristina Mancini,
Jason Young, Ryan Jones, Joshua Izzo, Nicole Spiegel, and Stephen Christy.

INTRODUCTION *BY JAMES DASHNER*

I had a life-defining moment when I was about ten years old. Miraculously, my mom let me spend the night at a friend's house. Who knew what sort of shenanigans might ensue? Well, my friend John pulled this huge box out of his closet, and it was bursting at the seams, full of comic books. Everything from *Spider-Man* to *Casper the Friendly Ghost*. So, instead of roaming the neighborhood that night like little demons, we stayed up all night reading those comics, devouring them until the sun came up.

It made me realize—traditional book nerd that I was—that there were other, just-as-cool ways to escape to another world for a time.

Storytelling. It's my favorite thing in the universe.

Books, comics, movies, music, theater—whatever form it may take. The escape of it, the journey, the heartbreak and laughs, the sheer entertainment of it all. I love when someone creates a world that becomes real to me in every way, whether it be an alternate version of this one, a far-off planet named Arrakis, a magical elfin land, or something I'd never be able to dream up myself. Like a playground, I love to go play in that world, release my imagination into its wonders for awhile.

The biggest accomplishment of my writing career has been creating a world in which millions of *others* have willingly found themselves lost. (It's still so hard to believe!) This has been the world of *The Maze Runner*—a future version of our own world that's bleak and harsh but still full of things like friendship, loyalty, and a fierce will to live. And characters that have become so real to so many. Seeing it all come to life on film—on the big screen—has been indescribably thrilling for me. Yes, I'm an author, but I could never find the right words.

Are there differences between the *Maze Runner* movies and the books? Of course. Having been involved from the beginning of the process, I supported

those changes from novel to film. It's a simple fact: some things that work on the page don't work in a movie, and vice versa. That's just the way it is. And it's okay! That's the great news! No one is more familiar with the novels than I am, and yet the films let me live that world and the characters in a way I never have before.

This is how I see the movies, side-stories, art, fan fiction, and the WCKD websites developed by the creative team behind the films. It's also how I see this new series of graphic novels depicting the events leading up to Thomas entering the Maze. Again, are there differences between "book canon" and "movie canon"? Certainly. But that's okay. Look at it as a means to experience parts of the story, or characters that you love, in a whole new way all over again. A way to enter the world and have it still feel fresh and new and exciting. (And, of course, terrifying.)

Like me, I hope you'll set aside any concerns over differences between these two versions of the same world. The characters you love are there, the spirit and tone and world structure are there. The differences are subtle enough to keep you on your toes and allow you to experience the roller coaster as if it's the first time you had the guts to step into the Maze, all over again. The books will always be there. Thomas, Alby, Teresa, Minho, Newt, Chuck, Gally—all of them live, and sometimes die, within those pages. Nothing ever *will* change within those volumes. Keep them on your shelves and open them up when you want those original, familiar moments.

Now, I invite you to step inside our playground for new adventures, new angles, new interpretations, new twists and turns. Familiar and different all at once. Come on in, and enjoy the ride.

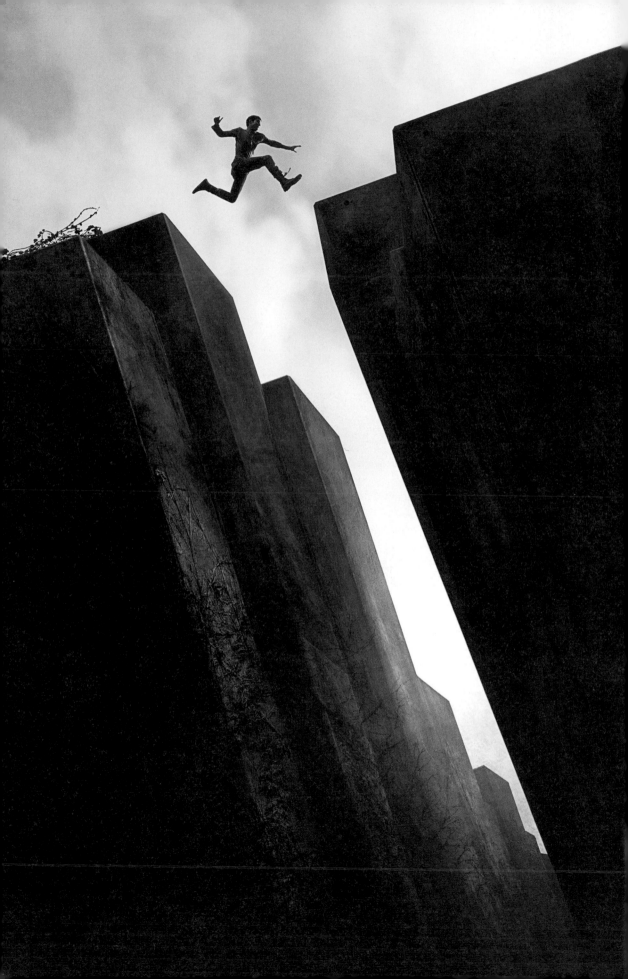

RUNNER'S JOURNAL. MINHO. DAY 401.

I LOST ANOTHER ONE TODAY.

POOR SHANK. THE DROPS GOT HIM.

GUESS I'M ON MY OWN TOMORROW.

RUNNING ON MY OWN.

GOOD. NOTHING TO SLOW ME DOWN.

DAY 430.

JUST GOT USED TO RUNNING ON MY OWN, NOW ALBY SAYS I HAVE TO TRAIN A NEW RUNNER. ONLY GONNA SLOW ME DOWN, BUT WHO ARGUES WITH ALBY?

BUT MAYBE HE'S RIGHT.

PLACE GOES ON FOREVER.

WHAT'S ANOTHER RUNNER CORPSE AT THE BOTTOM OF SOME DROP?

RUNNER'S JOURNAL.
MINHO. DAY 431.
PLANT YOUR FEET. WATCH YOUR LANDING.
MOVE FAST, BUT NEVER SLOPPY.
KEEP YOUR SHUCKIN' MOUTH SHUT.
THE KID IS SO GREEN I COULD LOSE HIM IN THE GRASS.

AFTER THAT, THE RUN WAS EASY.
CLEARING THAT WALL OPENED UP A NEW PATH.
AND EVERYONE BACK IN THE GLADE-- THEY WON'T BELIEVE WHAT WE FOUND.
A CLUE. A SIGN OF HOPE. ACTUAL HOPE.
A LIGHT AT THE END OF THE TUNNEL.

THE TRUE MAZE

ON THE MARCH TO THE TREE, I LEARN SOME BASICS.

THE GIRLS CALL THEMSELVES *ICERS*. THERE'S EIGHT OF THEM, TRAPPED HERE THE SAME AS I AM.

THEY CALL THIS PLACE THE *SPRING*. WALLS AROUND IT IN EVERY DIRECTION. THEY OPEN EVERY MORNING, CLOSE EVERY NIGHT.

EVERYTHING BEYOND IS *MAZE*.

ALSO? THEY ARE NOT EXACTLY *TRUSTING*.

OVER TWO YEARS SINCE I GOT DROPPED INTO THIS PLACE AND I AIN'T *NEVER* SEEN A BOY!

HE'S THE LAST ONE EVER. THAT'S WHAT IT SAYS, THIS NOTE THAT WAS PINNED ON HIS SHIRT.

NONE OF US HAVE. EVERY MONTH, LIKE CLOCKWORK, IT'S A NEW GIRL. AND NOW, ALL OF A SUDDEN, *THIS THING* ARRIVES?

I DON'T TRUST IT. WASN'T BORN YESTERDAY. HE'S A *SPY*. A *JINX*.

THE LAST ONE OF *US*. LOOK AT HIM, XIMENA! HE'S JUST AS CONFUSED AS ANY OF US WHEN WE ARRIVED!

POINT OF ORDER.

I SAY WE THROW HIM IN THE ICE AND LET THE SHADES TAKE HIM.

ABSOLUTELY *NOT!*

THAT'S NOT HOW WE *DO* THINGS, ALEJANDRA. *ICERS* WORK *TOGETHER*, AND WE LEAVE NO GIRL BEHIND.

'CEPT HE AIN'T A GIRL.

YOU THROW HIM TO THE ICE, YOU GO THROUGH ME.

AND REMEMBER WHAT HAPPENED TO THE *LAST* THING THAT TRIED TO TAKE ME ON.

WHICH IS WHEN I SEE IT.

THE SHADE.

OR AT LEAST THE BODY OF ONE.

I REMEMBER A **LOT** OF ANIMALS, EVEN IF I CAN'T REMEMBER SEEING THEM BEFORE. BIRDS. BATS. BEES.

BUT THE ONLY WORD I KNOW FOR THIS IS **MONSTER**.

RACHEL, YOU SAY ONE MORE THING ABOUT THAT SHADE YOU BAGGED AND I SWEAR TO THE **MAZE** I WILL BEAT YOU SO HARD THEY'LL HAVE TO **HANG YOU UP** NEXT TO IT.

THIS IS A DEMOCRACY. YOUR MIGHT DON'T MAKE RIGHT.

KILLING AN INNOCENT--BOY OR NOT--THAT'S WHAT ISN'T RIGHT!

YOU WANNA THROW DOWN, XIMENA?

IF THAT'S WHAT KEEPS US FROM BECOMING MURDERERS, THEN COME GET SOME--

EXCUSE ME.

WHAT?

XIMENA, YOU'RE **RIGHT**. YOU HAVE NO REASON TO TRUST ME. BUT RACHEL? YOU'RE **ALSO RIGHT**.

I'M NOT A SPY. I'M NOT HERE TO HURT YOU. SHUCK, I DON'T EVEN **KNOW** WHY I'M HERE, WHICH I THINK YOU ALL CAN RELATE TO. I'M NOT A **GIRL**, BUT THAT DOESN'T MEAN I'M YOUR ENEMY.

I DON'T REMEMBER WHO I AM, BUT I KNOW SOME THINGS. I KNOW I'M SMART. I KNOW I **WANT** TO HELP YOU.

PLEASE DON'T LEAVE ME BEHIND.

LET ME JOIN YOU.

HUH.

IT WORKED.

NICE SPEECH, NEW KID.

WHY... WHY DID YOU--?

CAN'T BE AN *ICER* UNTIL YOU REMEMBER YOUR *NAME.* BEEN AROUND LONG ENOUGH TO KNOW THAT THIS IS THE EASIEST WAY.

SO WHAT'S YOUR NAME?

I...MY NAME...

YOU NEED ME TO HIT YOU AGAIN, DUMBASS?

NO. STOP.

MY NAME IS *ARIS.*

EVERY MORNING IN THE SPRING IS EXACTLY THE SAME. A SCIENCE BORN FROM MORE THAN TWENTY MONTHS IN THE MAZE.

AS SOON AS THE SUN COMES OVER THE PEAK, THE GIRLS START **MAPPING.**

ONE OF THE ONLY SUPPLIES THEY HAVE IN SURPLUS IS PAPER. THEY MAKE CHARCOAL BY BURNING BRANCHES FROM THE DECISION TREE.

AND THOUGH THE MAZE CHANGES EVERY DAY, THEY CAN SEE THE HIGHER LEVELS OF THE MAZE FROM THE SPRING.

RACHEL AND SONYA ARE THE BEST MAPPERS ON THE TEAM. IT'S LIKE THEY CAN RUN THE MAZE IN THEIR HEADS.

WITH THE MAP IN HAND, THE WHOLE COMMUNITY PREPARES TOGETHER.

A TEAM, EACH WITH THEIR OWN STRENGTHS.

ROUTINE. GOOD FOR SURVIVAL AND PERSISTENCE.

EIGHT HARDENED SURVIVORS...AND ME.

I SAY I CAN KEEP UP. I HOPE IT'S TRUE. I NEED TO BELIEVE IT'S TRUE.

SO WHEN THE DOORS OPEN THE NEXT MORNING, I GATHER WITH THE REST. XIMENA LEADS THE COUNTDOWN.

ON **THREE,** THE ICERS DO WHAT THEY DO BEST...

AND I TRY TO KEEP UP.

COME **ON**, GIRLS! LET'S **PUSH** IT! SUMMIT'S JUST AROUND THE BEND.

SONYA, YOU'RE ON **POINT**. HARRIET...

MAKE THE THROW!

SWSSH

A PRACTICED MOVE.

SIMPLE.

FLAWLESS.

FOR A MOMENT, I'M RELIEVED.

BUT THEN I REALIZE THAT THE TRUE MAZE HASN'T EVEN BEGUN.

MAP CHECK!

TWO MORE BLOCKS *UP*, THEN WE SHIFT *RIGHT*. UP *ONE MORE* AND WE'RE AT THE PEAK.

NEVER GOTTEN THIS CLOSE. THINK THE SHADES ARE TAKING THE DAY OFF?

I THINK THEY'RE WAITING FOR US TO SLIP UP. SHADES KEEP THE EDGE OF THE MAZE AND THEY DO IT WELL. NEVER REACHED THE TOP, THEY'RE THE REASON WHY.

REMEMBER THAT, *ICERS*, AND KEEP AN EAR TO THE SKY.

DON'T WORRY, ARIS. SHADES COME SWOOPING DOWN, I'LL LET 'EM EAT YOU *FIRST*.

WHICH IS WHEN I START TO FEEL IT.

MUSCLE FAILURE.

ARIS? YOU OKAY, KID?

I'M...I'M OKAY! I CAN KEEP GOING! HOW MUCH LONGER?

LIKE I JUST SAID...

WE'RE ALMOST AT THE PEAK.

WE'VE NEVER GOTTEN THIS FAR BEFORE. YOU'RE OUR GOOD LUCK CHARM, ARIS!

SHUT YOUR HOLE, RACHEL. AIN'T NO SUCH THING AS LUCK.

JUST KEEP CLIMBING.

THRAK

RACHEL? RACHEL?

FOCUS ON MY VOICE. WE'RE GONNA GET YOU BACK TO THE SPRING. YOU'RE GONNA BE FINE.

I AM LYING AND I KNOW IT.

HER LEGS ARE GONE. SPLINTERS. EVEN IF SHE LIVES...

SHE'LL NEVER RUN AGAIN.

XIMENA WAS THE FIRST OF THEM. SPENT A MONTH HERE ALONE AND WELCOMED EVERY GIRL AFTER. EVERY ICER HAS A STORY.

IT'S A BEAUTIFUL MEMORIAL.

THAT TIME SHE LEAPED TWO BLOCKS IN A SINGLE JUMP. THAT TIME SHE FREE-CLIMBED TO SAVE HARRIET'S LIFE. THAT TIME SHE TRIED TO MAKE A FEAST OUT OF THE ALGAE THAT GROWS IN THE MAZE, ONLY TO GIVE THE WHOLE SPRING FOOD POISONING.

XIMENA

AND IT'S ALL MY FAULT.

BECAUSE I TRIED TO BE SOMETHING I'M NOT. A RUNNER. AN ICER.

WHOEVER I WAS BEFORE I CAME HERE? THAT KID MAY HAVE BEEN CLEVER, BUT HE SUCKED AT SPORTS. AND NOW A GIRL IS DEAD.

RACHEL WILL BE SORRY SHE EVER STOOD UP FOR ME. HER COMPASSION LEFT HER LYING THERE WHEN IT SHOULD HAVE BEEN ME.

I HAVE NO FRIENDS, NO FAMILY, NO MEMORY, AND NO PURPOSE.

ALL I CAN DO IS STARE AT THE MONSTER AND HOPE IT'LL WAKE LONG ENOUGH TO END ME.

WHICH IS WHEN I SEE IT.

AT FIRST THE NOTION SEEMS ABSURD, BUT INSPECTION ONLY CORROBORATES MY THINKING.

A PATTERN ON THE UNDERSIDE OF THE WINGS, PALE PINK CROSSED WITH DARK BLACK LINES.

NOT JUST VEINS, THOUGH THAT'S WHAT THEY'D APPEAR TO BE. SOMETHING MUCH STRANGER.

ANGULAR TURNS. WHEELS WITHIN WHEELS. CIRCUITS LEADING IN CONFUSING PATTERNS.

ONE ENTRANCE. ONE END POINT.

A MAZE.

THIS IS THE MISSING PIECE. JUST LIKE THAT, IT ALL MAKES SENSE.

THE SHADES DON'T PROTECT THE END OF THE MAZE.

THE SHADES ARE THE END OF THE MAZE.

I'M GONNA NEED PAPER. LOTS AND LOTS OF PAPER.

THE ICERS GATHER THE NEXT MORNING, MOSTLY TO MAKE SURE RACHEL KNOWS THAT EVEN THOUGH SHE CAN'T RUN, SHE'S STILL ONE OF THEM.

THEY WON'T EVEN LOOK AT ME.

WHEN SHE SEES THE MAP, I SWEAR HER SMILE COULD LIGHT UP THE SPRING.

SHE'S A NATURAL. PRACTICED AND DRIVEN BY INSTINCT.

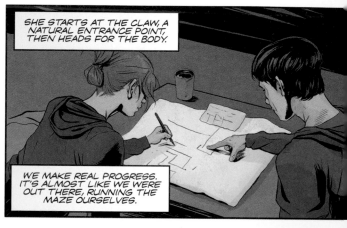

SHE STARTS AT THE CLAW, A NATURAL ENTRANCE POINT, THEN HEADS FOR THE BODY.

WE MAKE REAL PROGRESS. IT'S ALMOST LIKE WE WERE OUT THERE, RUNNING THE MAZE OURSELVES.

EVERY DAY, AFTER THEY LEAVE FOR THE ICE AGAIN, I DRAW THE NEXT PART OF THE PATTERN.

AND RACHEL RUNS IT LIKE AN EXPERT.

WE MAKE A GOOD TEAM. AND FOR ONCE, I FEEL LIKE I'M ACTUALLY GOOD AT SOMETHING.

BUT FOR EVERY BIT OF PROGRESS WE MAKE, THE SHADES IN THE MAZE GET BOLDER.

THE ICERS DON'T EVEN MAKE IT TO THE SUMMIT ANYMORE. THE ICE IS ONLY DEATH NOW.

BUT **SHE** DOES, WITH THE SAME KINDNESS AS BEFORE HER FALL.

YOU KNOW, YOU DON'T NEED TO DOTE ON ME. THIS ISN'T YOUR FAULT. YOU BROKE MY FALL.

IF WE'RE GONNA BE STUCK HERE TOGETHER, CAN YOU AT LEAST DROP THE SAD SACK ROUTINE AND LET THE PAST BE THE PAST?

I TELL HER I CAN.

I TELL HER WE HAVE **WORK** TO DO.

ALMOST.

WE MAKE GOOD PARTNERS.

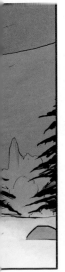

OUR ONLY HOPE IS THAT WHEREVER THIS LEADS US...

WHATEVER IS INSIDE THIS SHADE, AT THE END OF THIS MAZE...

OUR ONLY HOPE IS THAT IT'S **WORTH** IT.

SQUELCH

WOW.

...WE WERE **RIGHT**.

RIGHT ABOUT **WHAT?**

AND **WHEN** EXACTLY WERE YOU PLANNING ON CLUEING IN THE REST OF US?

SONYA, HARRIET--

SO MUCH FOR THE **TEAM**, HUH, RACHEL?

YOU WEREN'T EVEN BEING **SUBTLE** ABOUT IT. THE ENTIRE PAPER SUPPLY IS GONE. WE CAN'T EVEN **TRY** TO MAP THE MAZE ANYMORE.

SO TELL US.

TELL US WHAT WE'RE GONNA DIE FOR.

ASK ME, IT LOOKS LIKE A TRANSMITTER. A WAY TO CALL FOR HELP. IT MIGHT BE OUR ONLY SHOT.

IT'S GOT A BUTTON, WHICH WE CAN TAKE A VOTE ON PUSHING. DECIDE **LIKE ICERS**. WHAT DO YOU--

NO.

ARIS IS RIGHT. THIS IS OUR ONLY SHOT.

WE'RE **TAKING** IT.

CLICK

SKRIIIIIIIIIIIIIIILLLE

THE SHADES. YOU JUST RANG THE DINNER BELL.

IT DIDN'T WORK.

WE DON'T KNOW THAT. WE DON'T KNOW WHAT'S *GOING TO HAPPEN.*

IT DIDN'T SAVE US. IT WAS JUST ANOTHER TRAP. I'M SO SORRY.

DON'T BE.

YOU DIDN'T SAVE US, SURE. BUT THE TWO OF YOU PUT AN END TO THIS FIGHT. WE'RE EITHER KILLING THOSE SHADES AND CLIMBING OUT OF THIS PLACE...

OR WE'RE DEAD. SIMPLE AS THAT.

SO DON'T BE SORRY. YOU DID FREE US, AFTER A FASHION.

HARRIET'S RIGHT.

NO MORE RUNNING. IT'S TIME WE TOOK A *STAND.*

TOGETHER.

TOGETHER.

IF I'M GOING TO DIE, I CAN'T THINK OF A BETTER WAY.

FOR A SECOND, IT LOOKS LIKE WE MIGHT HAVE A CHANCE.

JUST A SINGLE SECOND.

RACHEL!

SKEEEEK

MY LAST DECISION.

MY LAST CHANCE.

THE LAST THING I'LL EVER SEE.

BEEP

WCKD

BLAM

IT WORKED. THE MAZE. THE TRANSMITTER. OUR LAST STAND.

IT WORKED.

HOLD ON, RACHEL.

WE'RE GONNA *GET OUT OF* HERE.

SURE YOU ARE, KID, BUT NOT LIKE THAT.

HOW 'BOUT WE GIVE YOU A *RIDE?*

COME ON, ICERS, KEEP IT UP!

SONYA AND HARRIET. PARTNERS UNTIL THE END.

I HOPE THEY'LL MAKE IT. I HOPE THEY'LL SURVIVE.

RACHEL AND I ARE PARTNERS, TOO. SO I DO MY PART.

AND I GET HER TO SAFETY.

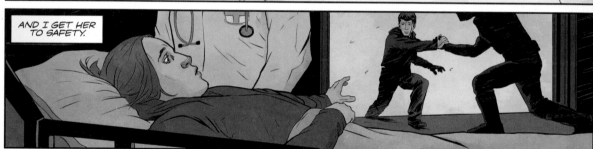

I TELL HER IT'LL BE ALRIGHT. I SEE IT IN HER EYES. LIKE SHE DOESN'T BELIEVE.

SO I SAY THE WORDS, OVER AND OVER AGAIN.

WE ARE SAFE. THE ONLY PEOPLE LEFT TO TELL THE TALE OF THE ICERS.

WE'RE SAFE.

WE'RE SAFE.

I'VE GOT **THREE** QUESTIONS.

WHERE DO YOU **COME** FROM?

STARTED IN PHOENIX. LOST OUR PARENTS OUTSIDE SALT LAKE. NO IDEA WHERE I AM NOW.

WHERE ARE YOU **GOING?**

THE FUTURE. ONE STEP AT A TIME.

HOW CAN I **PROFIT?**

WHAT KIND OF QUESTION IS THAT?

THE SIMPLE KIND?

...

I DON'T HAVE ANYTHING TO TRADE.

THEN I'M GONE.

AND WE'RE DONE.

YOU KNOW, WHEN THE CRANKS GET ME TONIGHT, I'M GONNA **SCREAM.**

I'VE SEEN 'EM DO IT, THEY'LL COME FROM MILES AROUND FOR A GOOD SCREAM, THAT'S HOW HUNGRY THEY ARE.

GOOD LUCK STAYING SAFE IN THE MIDDLE OF A SWARM.

...

ONE **NIGHT.** I'LL KEEP YOU ALIVE FOR **ONE NIGHT.**

WHY NOT A CELL? GOTTA BE MORE SECURE, RIGHT?

NEVER SLEEP ANYWHERE WITH ONLY ONE EXIT.

THAT **CRANK GUARD DOG** YOU SET OUTSIDE? THAT WAS SMART, I'LL GIVE YOU THAT.

BUT AN ALARM AIN'T WORTH DIRT IF YOU GOT NOWHERE TO RUN.

WHAT HAPPENS TOMORROW?

I MEAN, GEORGE AND I USED TO TAKE TURNS KEEPING WATCH. IF I'M ALONE...

GEORGE?

MY BROTHER.

...MY NAME IS JORGE.

I'M BRENDA.

AND IF YOU'RE NOT GOING TO TAKE ME WITH YOU, SEEMS TO ME YOU AT LEAST HAVE TO LEAVE ME SOMEWHERE SAFE.

OR OF COURSE YOU COULD JUST SHOOT ME YOURSELF.

KINDA HOPING AGAINST THAT OPTION, THOUGH.

NOWHERE IS SAFE.

BUT I KNOW A PLACE THAT'S TRYING.

WHERE IS THIS PLACE?

THE PEOPLE WE'RE LOOKING FOR TEND TO MOVE. OUTPOSTS EVERYWHERE. SO I DON'T KNOW.

KA KAW.

HANDS IN THE SKY. TREAD SLOW.

DAMN, JORGE. YOU ALMOST ENDED UP WITH A BELLY FULL OF CRANK REPELLENT.

THAT CLUNKER BREAK DOWN ON YOU YET?

YOU KNOW THAT THING SURVIVED WORSE THAN THIS. FINALLY CHANGE YOUR MIND ABOUT JOINING UP?

NEVER HAVE. NEVER WILL.

BUT THIS ONE WANTS TO MEET THE RIGHT ARM.

MARCUS. YOU KNOW YOU'RE NOT SUPPOSED TO VISIT OUR OUTPOSTS.

OH, I KNOW. BUT AN OLD FRIEND CAME KNOCKING.

JORGE. YOU'RE AN INSPIRATION. FINALLY DECIDED TO ACCEPT MY OFFER?

NO. NOT HERE FOR ME. THIS IS BRENDA.

HI THERE, BRENDA.

DO YOU LIKE PAD SEE EW?

FAMILY?

DEAD. WCKD TOOK HER BROTHER.

SHE'S IN SHOCK, BUT SHE DOESN'T KNOW IT YET.

CAN YOU BLAME HER?

I CANNOT. BUT I ALSO CAN'T HAVE HER SLOWING ME DOWN.

THIS LIFE IS RISKY ENOUGH WITHOUT THAT KIND OF TROUBLE.

YOU EVER GET THE FEELING THE WORLD IS OUT TO GET YOU?

I'VE BEEN RUNNIN' SO LONG, I DON'T KNOW IF I'M THINKING STRAIGHT. I DON'T...

...THEY GOT WATER, AND SHELTER. MARY SEEMS NICE. AND THOSE *NOODLES*.

BUT I DON'T TRUST ANY OF IT.

THE WORLD *CAN'T* BE OUT TO GET YOU.

FOR THAT TO BE TRUE, THE WORLD WOULD HAVE TO CARE. *AND IT DOESN'T*.

NOT ABOUT YOU. CERTAINLY NOT ABOUT ME. THIS WORLD TRIED TO BURN US OFF AND WE'RE THE UNLUCKY ONES THAT SURVIVED. SO IF THE RIGHT ARM CAN GIVE YOU SOMETHING TO LIVE FOR, EVEN IF IT'S A GOOD MEAL, THEN I'D--

--hell.

THU THU THU THU THU

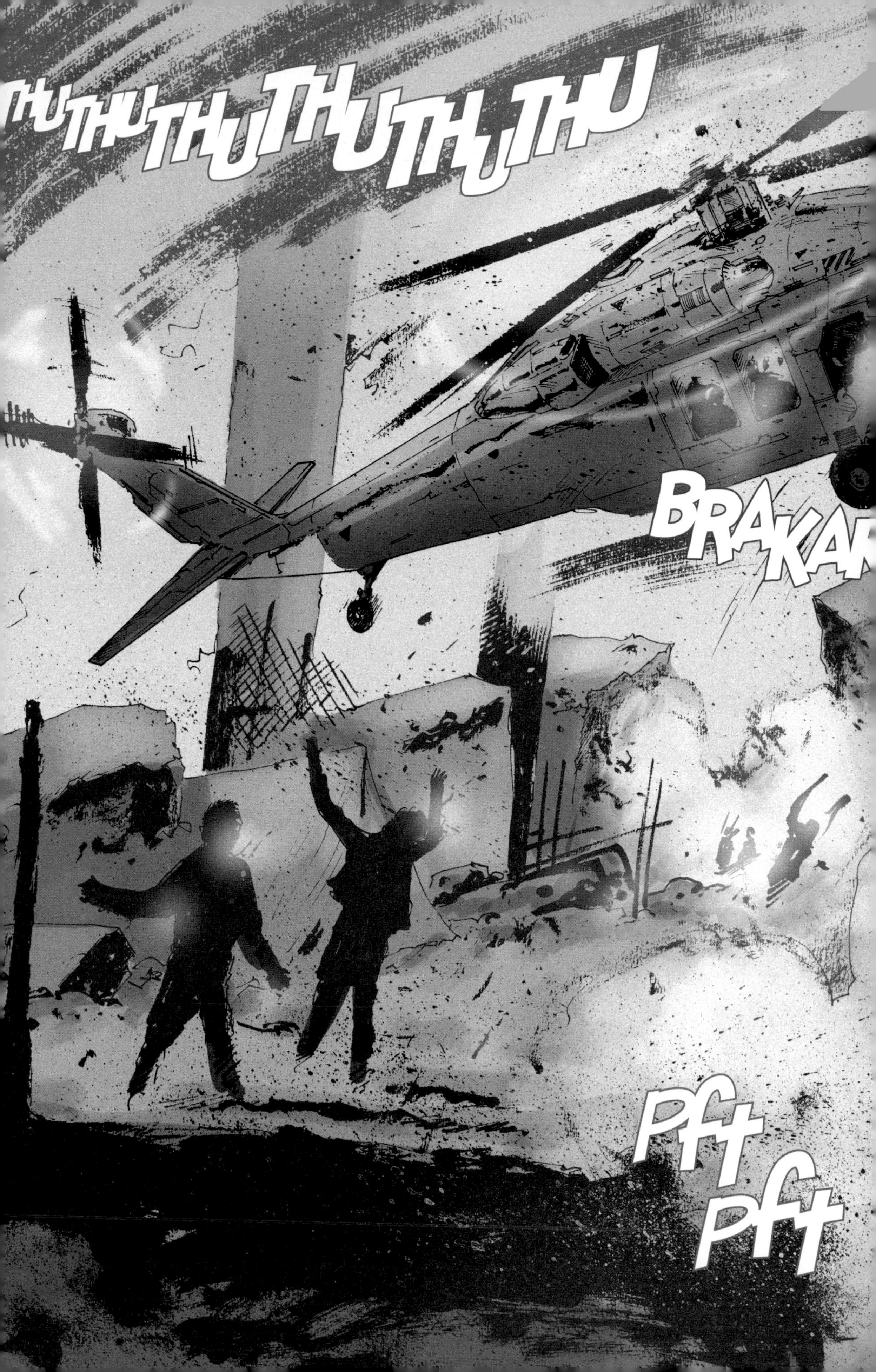
THUTHUTHUTHUTHUTHU
BRAKAK
PFT PFT

PRIORITIZE ANYONE AT STAGE THREE. CARRY THEM IF YOU HAVE TO.

STAGE ONES, HELP THE TWOS.

LEAVE THE GEAR, WE HAVE MORE AT *CENTRAL COMMAND*.

MARY, WHAT IS THIS?

WE'RE *SAVING THE WORLD*, JORGE.

DID YOU THINK WE WERE GOING TO DO IT WITH GUNS?

THE FLARE IS IN OUR BRAINS.

WE'RE ALL CRANKS, JUST SOME OF US DON'T REALIZE IT YET.

BUT SOME OF THESE KIDS ARE *IMMUNE*.

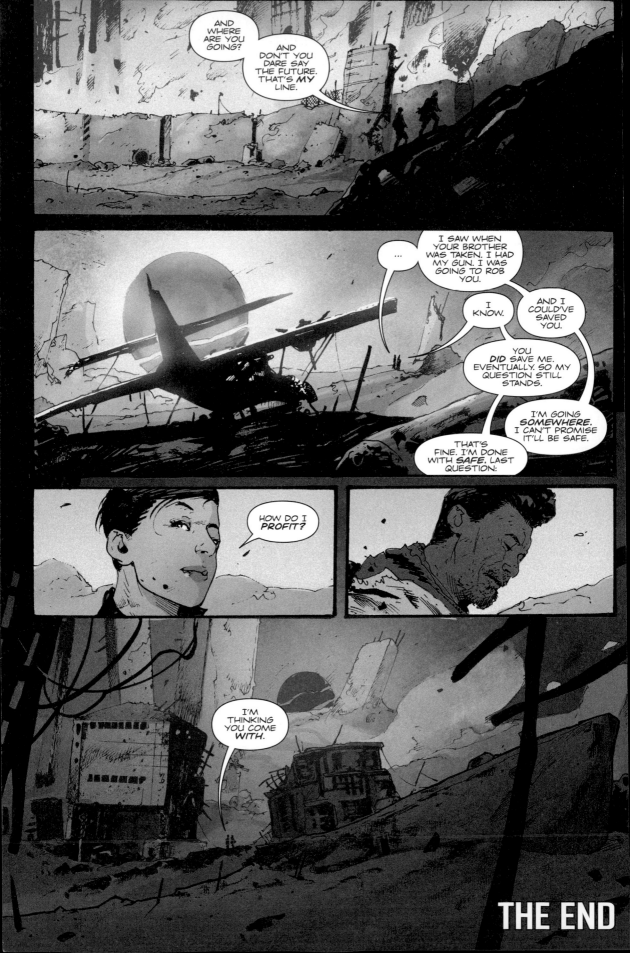

THE END

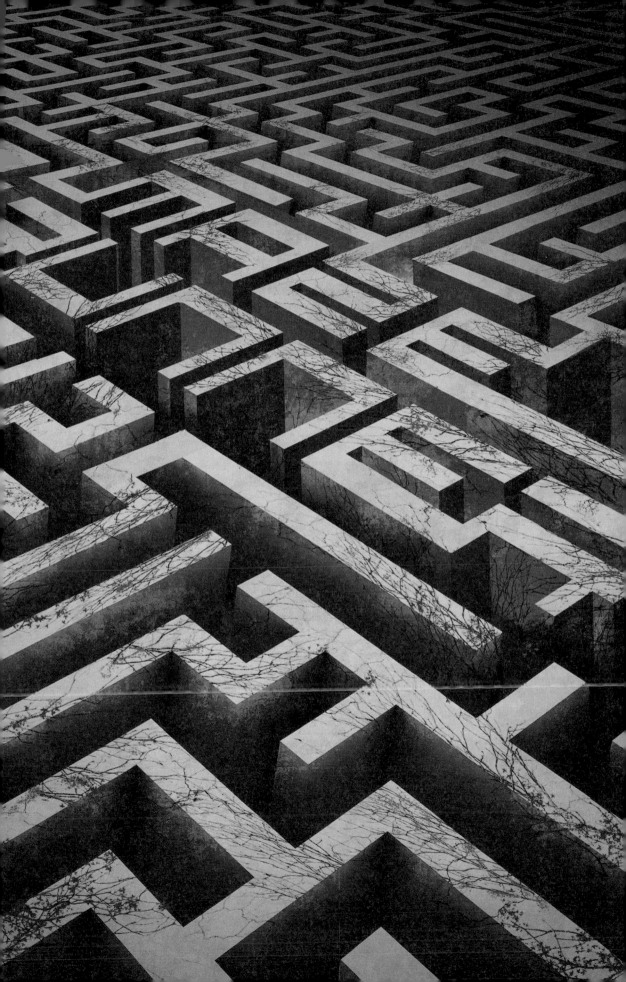

FOUR AND A HALF **BILLION** DEAD IN LESS THAN **FIFTEEN MINUTES**.

AND STILL THERE ARE TOO MANY OF US.

POST-FLARE COALITION GOVERNMENT SPECIAL RESOURCE CONFERENCE, SIX MONTHS AFTER THE Z136 SOLAR FLARE.

THE SURVEYS REQUESTED BY THIS BODY HAVE BEEN COMPLETED.

SUFFICE TO SAY, THE PROGNOSIS IS EXTREMELY **GRIM**. NEARLY EVERY CROP THAT ONCE GREW ON EARTH IS NOW EXTINCT DUE TO THE INCREASED RADIATION AND CHANGED CLIMATES.

MEXICO AND INDIA ARE BURNED OFF THE MAP. AMERICAN FARMS ARE DYING. EUROPE IS UNDER WATER. THAT DOESN'T JUST MEAN THAT IT'S **RUSSIA'S LUCKY DAY**.

IT MEANS WE ARE RUNNING OUT OF **FOOD, DRINKABLE WATER,** AND **SHELTER**.

EXCUSE ME, MR. JANSON. **AVA PAIGE**, FORMER UNITED STATES.

WHEN YOU SAY WE'RE **RUNNING OUT**, WHAT YOU ACTUALLY MEAN IS THAT WE HAVE SUSTAINABLE RESOURCES FOR ONLY **SEVENTY PERCENT** OF THE REMAINING POPULATION, ISN'T THAT RIGHT?

THEY'RE EQUIVALENT SITUATIONS, MS. PAIGE.

NOT TO MY EARS.

I AGREE.

HI. I'M DR. MARY COOPER WITH THE PFC SCIENTIFIC INITIATIVE.

IF YOU'VE GOT ENOUGH FOR SEVENTY, THEN YOU'VE GOT ENOUGH FOR **EVERYONE**. I DON'T SEE ANY MENTION OF **RATIONING** IN YOUR PROPOSAL. I THINK IF WE FOLLOW MS. PAIGE'S LEAD--

DR. COOPER. I THINK YOU MISUNDERSTAND ME.

RATIONING WILL TRIGGER RIOTS. FACTIONING. MAYBE EVEN WAR. IT COULD FRACTURE THIS VERY COALITION.

THE SOLUTION IS SOMETHING MUCH SIMPLER. YOU'RE A SCIENTIST, SO LOOK AT THE MATH.

SAY WE HAVE **ONE HUNDRED PEOPLE**. WE HAVE FOOD ENOUGH FOR **SEVENTY**.

WE NEED TO SUBTRACT THE EXCESS **THIRTY**.

MONTH ONE.

MONTH TWO.

BEWARE THE FLARE
WASH YOUR HANDS
AND WEAR YOUR MASK

MONTH SEVEN.

MONTH TWELVE.

MUTATION.

A SIMPLE MUTATION.

THE PEOPLE HAVE STARTED CALLING THEM CRANKS.

WE HAVE OCCURRENCES IN MOST MAJOR POPULATION CENTERS. FORTUNATELY, THE SCORCH IS SLOWING THEM DOWN--FIRST GOOD THING THE FLARES HAVE DONE FOR US.

MEANS WE HAVE TIME TO FIX THIS.

DR. COOPER. MARY.

YOU AND I BOTH KNOW THAT YOU'RE THE ONLY ONE WHO CAN GET IT UNDER CONTROL. IF YOU CAN'T TELL THE PFC YOUR FINDINGS, THEN TELL ME.

THAT SAMPLE. THE ONE YOU CAN'T STOP EYEING. IT MEANS SOMETHING, I KNOW IT DOES.

...

I FOUND AN IMMUNITY.

AN IMMUNITY IN CHILDREN.

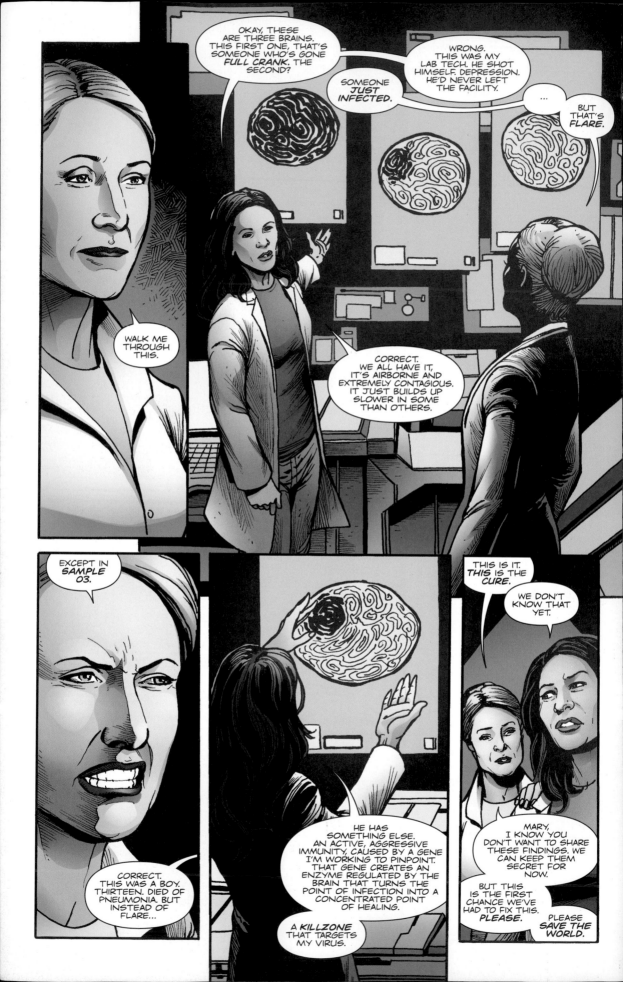

FOUR WEEKS IN AND THE KIDS ARE STILL HEALTHY. WELL, I MEAN, THEY HAVE ABOUT FOUR DOZEN CHILDHOOD ILLNESSES BETWEEN THEM, BUT NOTHING THAT WILL AFFECT THE TESTS.

THE RESULT OF THE EXTREME CONDITIONS BEYOND OUR WALLS.

I CAN FEEL IT. A CHANCE TO COURSE CORRECT.

THESE CHILDREN ARE THE VERY DEFINITION OF HOPE.

THEY BARELY GOT THE CHANCE TO KNOW THE WORLD THAT WAS.

NOW THEY WILL.

MARY COOPER, YOU MESSED UP.

BUT YOU HAVEN'T WASHED OUT.

NOT YET.

YOU'RE STILL IN THE FIGHT.

DR. COOPER. CONGRATULATIONS ON YOUR **BREAKTHROUGH.** I HEAR YOU MIGHT VERY WELL SAVE US ALL.

WHAT THE HELL IS GOING ON HERE?

SIT DOWN. THIS'LL ONLY TAKE A MINUTE.

DOCTOR MARY COOPER, THE GENIUS WHO'S GOING TO SAVE US FROM THE FLARE.

AND YOUR NAME IS--

NOT IMPORTANT. FRANKLY, I'M MUCH MORE INTERESTED IN **YOURS.**

SO, THE PLAN IS TO CONFISCATE A LARGE PERCENTAGE OF THE WORLD'S POTENTIALLY IMMUNE CHILDREN, BECAUSE WHAT'S INSIDE THEIR BRAINS COULD SAVE THE HUMAN RACE.

THE PFC CAN'T DO THIS, OF COURSE. THEY DON'T HAVE THE AUTHORITY AND FRANKLY, THEIR **IMAGE** ONLY HURTS YOU. THE WORLD IS DYING UNDER THEIR COMMAND.

SO HERE'S WHAT YOU DO. YOU'RE **NOT** THE PFC, THEY'RE JUST THE EGG FROM WHICH YOU WERE BIRTHED.

YOU ARE THE WORLD CATASTROPHE KILLZONE DEPARTMENT.

YOU **RECOGNIZE** THAT OUR PLANET'S AT **RISK** AND YOU HAVE EXACTLY **ONE PURPOSE:** EXPLOITING THE SO-CALLED **KILLZONE.** EASY RECOGNITION, EASY TRUST.

OF COURSE, THE NAME'S A BIT OF A **MOUTHFUL,** I **AGREE.** AND THE ACRONYM, REGRETTABLY, REMINDS ONE OF, SAY, A CHILD-STEALING **WITCH.**

SO WE'LL JUST REPEAT THE SLOGAN UNTIL IT STICKS.

THE SLOGAN?

WICKED.

IS.

GOOD.

THESE STEPS WERE ALWAYS NECESSARY, BUT THE OUTPOURING OF SACRIFICE HAS MADE IT *NOBLE*.

I AM TOLD BY GENERAL *JANSON* THAT BEYOND THE *VOLUNTEERS*, OUR BRAVE BOYS RESCUED MANY YOUNG ORPHANS IN THE LAST TWELVE MONTHS. THOSE THAT THE P.F.C. COULD NOT CARE FOR, WE WILL RAISE AS *OUR OWN*.

WE WILL FIND A *CURE*, EVEN IF IT TAKES US A *YEAR*.

WE ASK THAT YOU REMAIN IN YOUR HOMES DURING THESE TROUBLED TIMES. KNOW THAT WE CONTINUE TO FIGHT FOR YOU, BUT DO NOT EXPECT SAFETY SOON.

AFTER ALL, GREAT BATTLES ARE *RARELY* QUICK.

WE HAVE FOUGHT TOO HARD TO LOSE.

WE WILL SEE THIS THROUGH.

AND WCKD WILL PREVAIL.

PEAK EFFECTIVITY 15%

YOU LOOK LIKE YOU COULD USE A DRINK.

I DON'T THINK THOSE EXIST ANYMORE.

I GOT LOST ONCE.

I WAS HIKING WITH MY FAMILY NEAR CRATERS OF THE MOON. WE GOT SEPARATED, AND I PANICKED.

I RACED NORTH, SOUTH, UP AND DOWN. ONLY MADE IT WORSE.

I FELL. GOT FROSTBIT. SUN WENT DOWN. THEN I PANICKED SO HARD I BLACKED OUT.

NEXT DAY, I TRY A DIFFERENT TACTIC. LEFT, RIGHT, EAST, WEST. FOR THREE DAYS.

IT TURNS OUT I HAD ONLY COVERED ABOUT THREE SQUARE MILES. BUT TO ME, IN THAT *WASTELAND*? EVERY PATH WAS ANOTHER CHANCE TO SURVIVE.

SO MAYBE WE SHOULD STOP CHASING SOMETHING WE CAN'T FIND.

WRONG LESSON. IF I WOULD HAVE STAYED PUT, I WOULD HAVE DIED OF HYPOTHERMIA.

WHAT I'M SAYING IS THAT SOMETIMES YOU DON'T KNOW WHERE YOU'RE GOING. YOU JUST HAVE TO GO.

I BELIEVE IN YOU, MARY. I DON'T HAVE AN ANSWER AND I KNOW YOU DON'T EITHER. NOT YET.

BUT THERE'S NO PUZZLE YOU CAN'T SOLVE.

NO MATTER HOW BIG.

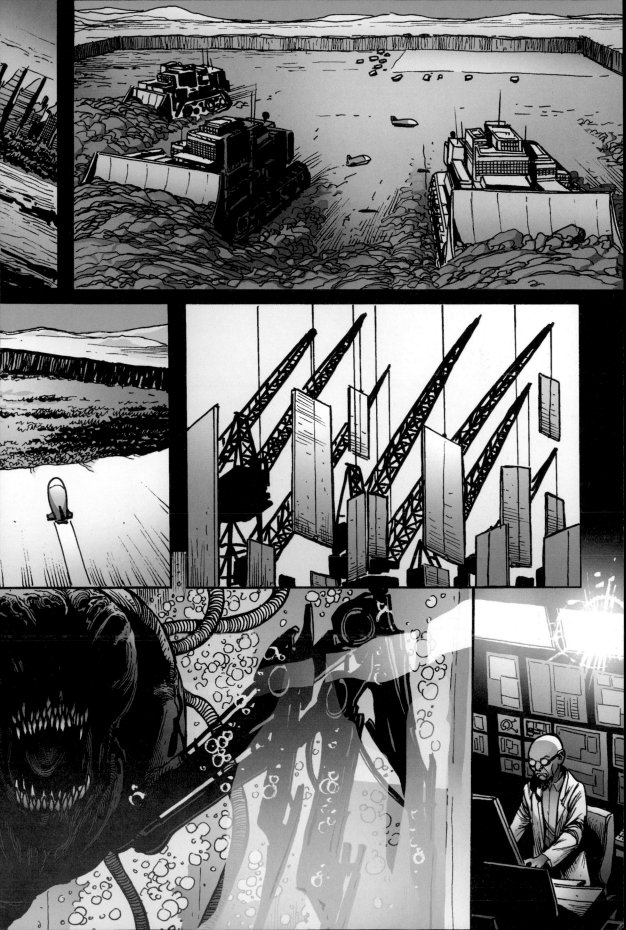

DEAR AVA.

YOU'RE RIGHT.

I WAS FOCUSED ON THE PROBLEM. AND ONLY THE PROBLEM.

I LET YOU CONVINCE ME TO DO TERRIBLE THINGS IN SERVICE OF THAT FOCUS. CONVINCED MYSELF THAT UP WAS DOWN.

THAT WICKED WAS GOOD.

BY THE TIME YOU READ THIS, I'LL HAVE TAKEN THE JEEP. I WON'T BE RETURNING IT, UNLESS IT'S TO DRIVE YOU DOWN.

FROM THIS DAY, YOU AND I ARE AT WAR.

YOUR MAZES WILL FALL. THOSE YOU PREY UPON WILL BE PROTECTED.

SIGNED, DR. MARY COOPER.

YOUR RIGHT ARM.

AND I WILL FIX THE MESS YOU MADE. I AM STILL IN THE FIGHT.

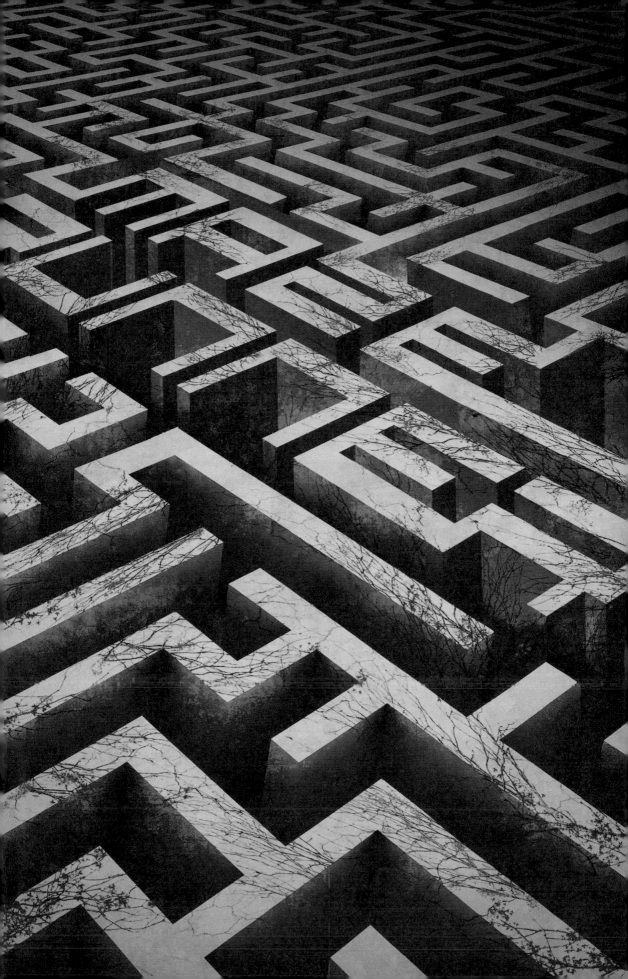

IF YOU LIKE *MAZE RUNNER* YOU'LL LOVE...

THE WOODS

On October 16, 2013, 437 students, 52 teachers, and 24 additional staff from Bay Point Preparatory High School in suburban Milwaukee, WI vanished without a trace. Countless light years away, far outside the bounds of the charted universe, 513 people find themselves in the middle of an ancient, primordial wilderness. Where are they? Why are they there? The answers will prove stranger than anyone could possibly imagine.

Created and written by James Tynion IV *(Batman Eternal)* and illustrated by Michael Dialynas *(Amala's Blade)*, each collection contains four issues of the best-selling series. Fans of teen conspiracy comics like *Morning Glories, Sheltered, and Revival*, will immediately be sucked into *The Woods*.

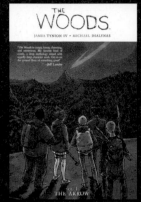 

THE WOODS VOL. 1 SOFTCOVER
978-1-60886-454-6

THE WOODS VOL. 2 SOFTCOVER
978-1-60886-495-9

HEXED

They say there is no honor among thieves—put that thief in the occult underground and you have a whole different kind of nasty. Traveling within the magical realm that lies beneath our own, thief-for-hire Luci Jennifer Inacio Das Neves—"Lucifer" for short—steals wondrous objects from the dark denizens of the netherworld. But when her latest job goes awry, can Lucifer save herself from being...hexed?

The adventure continues when Lucifer accidentally unleashes a terrible evil from one of her stolen paintings, will any of the tricks up her sleeve be enough to stop it? Created and written by Michael Alan Nelson *(Day Men, 28 Days Later)* and illustrated by the talents of Emma Rios *(Pretty Deadly)* and newcomer Dan Mora, Lucifer's story is only just beginning.

HEXED SOFTCOVER
978-1-60886-045-6

HEXED VOL. 1 SOFTCOVER
978-1-60886-718-9

SUICIDE RISK

Super-powered people are inexplicably rising from the streets and there's a big problem: Too many supervillains, not enough superheroes. Heroes are dying, and cops are dying twofold. Humanity is under-powered and good people are suffering untold tragedies trying to stem the flow. Beat cop Leo Winters is one of those struggling to make a difference. And the answer just might come in the form of two lowlifes with a dark secret.

The critically-acclaimed series by award-winning author Mike Carey *(X-Men, The Unwritten)* and fan-favorite artist Elena Casagrande *(Hulk, Hack/Slash)*. *Suicide Risk* is a high octane, mind-bending series created by one of the comic book industry's greatest storytellers.

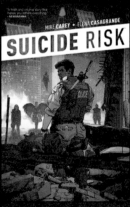 

SUICIDE RISK VOL. 1 SOFTCOVER
978-1-60886-332-7

SUICIDE RISK VOL. 2 SOFTCOVER
978-1-60886-360-0